INTRODUCTION

Although little evidence remains today, for a century between the 1860s a[nd] important secondary railway centre. Like many other railway centres, Oswe[stry's] railway network was brought about more by the rivalry between various comp[anies] to control potential traffic flows, in this case between England and Mid Wales, t[han the] transport needs of the people and businesses of Oswestry.

The development of the various lines in the Oswestry area is outlined in the following chapters. However, it is clear that the decision of the Cambrian Railways, formed in 1864 by the amalgamation of the Oswestry & Newtown, Oswestry, Ellesmere & Whitchurch, Llanidloes & Newtown and Newtown & Machynlleth Railways, to establish their headquarters at Oswestry that made it a railway town for the next hundred years. The growth of the town's population, from 5,414 in 1861 to 7,306 in 1871 and 9,479 in 1901 was undoubtedly due at least in part to the coming of the railways.

Although Oswestry's importance has been noted in words and pictures in a number of other railway books, particularly those on aspects of the Cambrian Railways, the compilers believe that this new collection of photographs capture something of the character of the area's railways. Mention of dates and Acts of Parliament have been kept to the essential minimum as they are easily obtained elsewhere.

Defining boundaries for the purposes of this book has been difficult; the boundaries of the town are rather limiting while the GWR's Oswestry District stretched as far as the Cambrian Coast and Brecon. The scope of this book therefore includes the Cambrian main line between Whitchurch and Welshpool, the Tanat Valley and Llanfyllin branches, the Shropshire & Montgomeryshire and industrial lines in the area in addition to Oswestry itself with its station, shed and works.

The compilers have tried to include all locations of interest but it is inevitable that there are some gaps, particularly industrial locations. Should readers wish to make contact with the compilers, especially if they have additional information or photographs, they may do so via the publisher.

Adrian Bodlander
Mark Hambly
Harry Leadbetter
Dave Southern

August 1994

Acknowledgments

The compilers wish to record their gratitude to all those who have helped in the preparation of this book, particularly all the photographers and collectors who have made their photographs available for publication. Special mention must be made of Mr Richard Casserley for allowing a number of his late father's photographs to be used, Norman Kneale for his interior views of Oswestry Works and Mike Lloyd for the information he provided on the Tanat Valley. The staff of the Shropshire Local Studies Library were also most helpful in locating photographs from their collection. It is appropriate to record our thanks to the various railwaymen whose cooperation ensured that photographs of the Blodwell Quarry ballast train were obtained while the tolerance of the staff at Blodwell Quarry and Llanforda Waterworks towards curious enthusiasts is also appreciated.

A private owner coal wagon built by the Midland Railway Carriage & Wagon Company for James Nurse, Coal Merchant, of Oswestry.
[*Shropshire Records & Research Unit*]

Bibliography

The following list, although not exhaustive, includes a number of the more significant works which cover railways in the Oswestry area.

Branch Line to Shrewsbury, V Mitchell & K Smith, Middleton Press.
The Cambrian Railways, R W Kidner, Oakwood Press.
Forgotten Railways - North & Mid Wales, Rex Christiansen, David & Charles.
Industrial Locomotives of Cheshire, Shropshire & Herefordshire, Industrial Railway Society.
Industrial Locomotives of North Wales, Industrial Railway Society.
Regional History of the Railways of Great Britain - North & Mid Wales, P E Baughan, David & Charles.
The Tanat Valley, W J Wren, David & Charles.
The Tanat Valley Railway, M E M Lloyd, Wild Swan.

Oswestry Station, Shed & Works

As noted in the introduction, Oswestry once possessed all the features of a major railway centre with a substantial station and adjacent yards, a locomotive shed and both locomotive and carriage & wagon works.

The Station

Oswestry's first station opened in December 1848 as the terminus of the Shrewsbury & Chester Railway's branch from Gobowen. This remained the railhead for Mid Wales until the Oswestry & Newtown Railway opened in 1861, its station in Oswestry being alongside but separate from that of the S&C which had become part of the GWR in 1854.

With the complete opening of the Oswestry, Ellesmere & Whitchurch Railway in July 1864 and the formation of the Cambrian Railways the same year the O&N station gained importance. 1866 saw the opening of the impressive Italianate style building housing both station and headquarters office facilities which remains to this day.

Following the amalgamation of the Cambrian Railways with the GWR in 1922 the GWR carried out various improvements to the Cambrian station including the addition of a new bay platform for Gobowen trains, the extension of the down platform and the removal of a ticket platform which had previously stood outside the station. As a result of the improvements Gobowen trains began using the Cambrian station from July 1924 although the GWR station was retained for goods use.

Through passenger trains on the former Cambrian main line ceased in January 1965 with those to Gobowen following in November 1966.

The Shed

The Oswestry & Newtown Railway opened a locomotive shed in the town in 1861, a facility which was to remain part of the town's railway scene through Cambrian, GWR and BR days until eventual closure in 1965.

The shed was the largest on the Cambrian system and was located north of the station in the fork between the Gobowen and Whitchurch lines. In parallel with their improvements to the station following amalgamation, the GWR also modernised the motive power depot facilities by installing electric lighting, additional inspection pits, improved roof ventilation and a standard GWR design coaling stage.

In 1947 the six road shed had an allocation of 36 locomotives, mostly of GWR origin but including three ex-Cambrian 2-4-0Ts retained for working the Tanat Valley. Even in 1961 there was still an allocation of some 30 locomotives of which over 20 were required to be in service to fulfil the daily workings for which the shed and its 100 enginemen were responsible.

The Works

The first initiative to build a works at Oswestry was taken in April 1863 when the Oswestry & Newtown Railway asked Benjamin Piercy, a prominent railway engineer of the day, to prepare plans for a repair shop and carriage works. By August of that year the O&N had agreed in principle to the works being built at a cost of £28,000. However, nothing happened.

By the time the Cambrian Railways came into being in July 1864 the need for a repair works was becoming urgent. At the Company's first board meeting Thomas Savin, the contractor responsible for the construction of the new Company's constituent railways, was asked to prepare specifications. The design was carried out by Manchester locomotive builders Sharp, Stewart & Company. At this time Savin had a small shop at Welshpool and this prompted the citizens of that town to urge the Cambrian board to locate their facility there in preference to Oswestry. The board were unmoved, however, and went ahead with the Oswestry scheme. Savin was awarded the contract to build the works which was equipped with Sharp, Stewart machinery. The works was in partial use by January 1866 when Savin's business empire failed and the Cambrian were obliged to complete the construction themselves. When the works opened fully in August 1866 the Welshpool shops closed.

Oswestry Works were built north east of the station in a part of the town known as the Shelf. The works were laid out as follows:

>At the west end were a gas oil works and the erecting shops;
>In the centre were offices, wash houses and the stores;
>At the east end were the carriage and wagon works and the paint shop.

The erecting shop had a central traverser serving twelve roads on each side including the entrance and the through road which were always kept clear. Other roads could accommodate a single locomotive and tender. Locomotives were moved by the tedious method of 'pinching' as far as the yard outside the shop where the works shunter took over. At the other end of the works a network of sidings fanned out across a yard and eleven roads, including the through road, entered the carriage and wagon shops. A two foot gauge tramway ran the length of the carriage & wagon works and out to a timber drying store.

Many new carriages and wagons were built at Oswestry but only two locomotives were ever built there. However, many extensive rebuilds were carried out.

Oswestry locomotive works saw a full century of service before finally being closed by British Railways on 31 December 1966, being the last GWR works to overhaul steam locomotives. The carriage & wagon works had closed two years previously during 1964.

1. Oswestry, 1955

An excellent view of the main building located on the Up side of the station. On the Cambrian main line the zero milepost was at Whitchurch so journeys towards Whitchurch were 'Up' and those away were 'Down'. As described in the text, this building with its commanding bay window and rows of chimneys was built as the headquarters of the Cambrian Railways. The sawtooth canopy on the Up side contrasts with the plain edged one on the Down. Another feature of note is the bracket signal mounted on top of the Up canopy with the arm of a backing signal just visible below the canopy. At the far end of the Up platform a train is waiting to depart for Whitchurch while a GWR 0-6-0PT is preparing to remove the two rear coaches.
[*Stations UK*]

2. Oswestry, 1931
Cambrian 2-4-0T 1196 shunts coaching stock on the middle road. Built in 1866 by Sharp, Stewart & Co of Manchester, these little tank engines spent the latter part of their working lives on the Tanat Valley line for which their light axle loading made them ideal. 1196 and sister 1197 were the last Cambrian tank engines to remain in service, just surviving into nationalisation.
[*A G Coltas*]

3. Oswestry, 1963
GWR 'Manor' 4-6-0 7800 *Torquay Manor* leaves the Down platform with a Whitchurch to Welshpool train. Note that the arrangement of signals at the end of the Up canopy has been altered from that shown in the two previous views.
[*E N Kneale*]

4. Oswestry, c.1963
GWR 'Manor' 4-6-0 7820 *Dinmore Manor* and 0-6-0PT 3668 stand at a bank of three ground signals on the centre road, presumably waiting to go 'onshed'. The various railwaymen present provide human interest.
[*E N Kneale*]

5. Oswestry, 1957
The Gobowen branch train stands in the bay platform formed of two different types of 'autocoach' headed by a GWR 0-6-0PT. The building just visible behind the goods wagons to the right of the locomotive is the GWR passenger station which closed in 1924. Note the large water tank behind the first coach which supplied the station water cranes.
[*N C Simmons*]

6. Oswestry, c.1957
Another view of the branch train in the bay platform with a clear view Down through the station at a quiet moment in the day's activities.
[*Lens of Sutton*]

7. Oswestry, 1964
The decline in traffic is now becoming noticeable with far fewer wagons in evidence at the goods station. GWR 0-6-0PT is shunting a few vans while the main line signal has been cleared for a train to Whitchurch. In the Gobowen bay the new order in the form of a 2 car DMU may be seen.
[*Mike Lloyd*]

8. Oswestry, c.1963
A different angle on the previous view with a variety of wagons present at the goods station and an unidentified 'Manor' taking water at the end of the Up platform.
[*E N Kneale*]

9 Oswestry, c.1963
GWR 'Manor' 4-6-0 7810 *Draycott Manor* is framed in the signal gantry at the north end of the station while working an Up train. The driver is leaning out of the cab watching the fireman whose conversation with a passenger at the leading window of the first coach is diverting him from 'putting the bag in'. The works chimney is a dominating feature on the skyline.
[*E N Kneale*]

10. Oswestry, c.1963
By turning 180 degrees this rarely seen view of the north end of the complex is obtained. The North signal box stands squarely in the centre with the Gobowen line to the left and the Whitchurch line to the right. To the left of the Gobowen line the sidings hold a train of ballast hoppers complete with plough brake van. The locomotive shed may be seen beyond and to the right of the signal box while on the extreme right is part of the works complex.
[*Tony Birch*]

11. Oswestry, 1926
A classic scene with GWR 4-4-0 1082, built at Oswestry in 1901 as Cambrian 19, passing under the north end signal gantry while a tank engine shunts freight wagons in the yard. The footbridge to the works is a prominent feature in the background.
[*The late H C Casserley*]

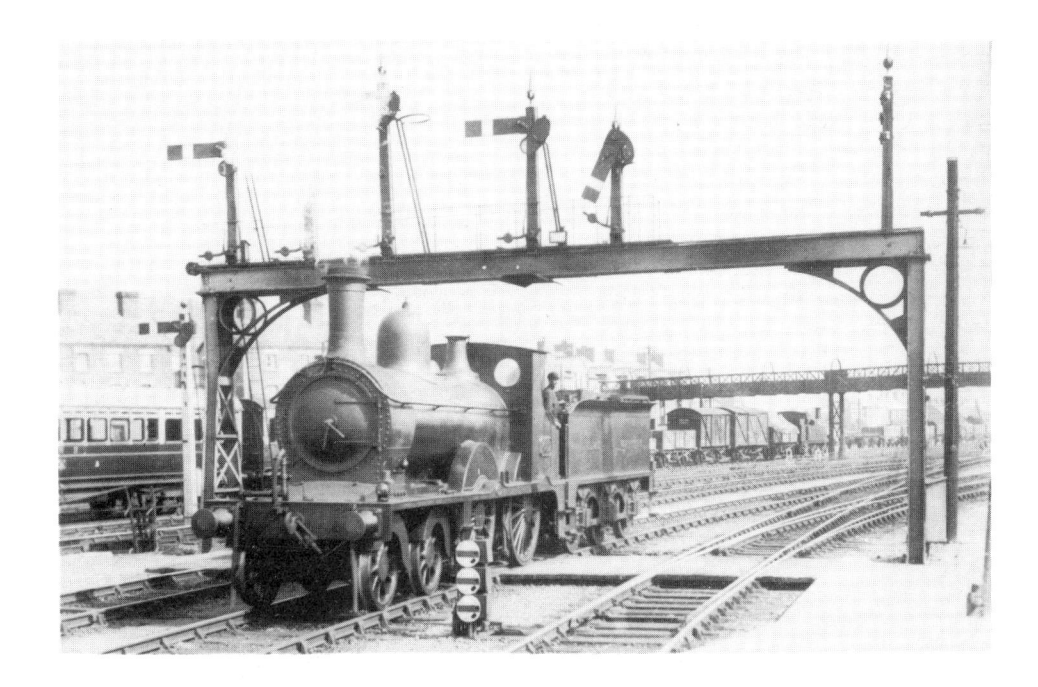

12. Oswestry, 1926
GWR 0-4-2T 574 shunts an assortment of wagons and vans in Oswestry yard. 574 was built in 1870 as a member of the 517 Class, a forerunner of the later 14xx Class.
[*The late H C Casserley*]

13. Oswestry, 1970
By the time this photograph was taken Oswestry South signal box was only handling goods traffic, through passenger trains having ceased in 1965. The sidings behind the box are still receiving coal wagons for the local merchant. The broken windows suggest that the box was only open for a few hours each day and subject to vandalism when closed. Happily the structure still exists as it and the coal yard are the base of the Cambrian Railways Society who hope eventually to operate a steam passenger service over part of the remaining line between Gobowen and Blodwell Junction.
[*Mike Lloyd*]

14. Oswestry, c.1970
D5143 departs for Gobowen. The gantry still looks impressive although both it and the ground signal have been rationalised to reflect the closure of the Whitchurch line. The footbridge and North signal box look little changed from earlier photographs.
[*E N Kneale*]

15. Oswestry Shed, c.1960
This view from the BR era shows the dramatic change in appearance brought to the shed by the GWR's 1939 roof renewal when elegant brickwork gave way to workaday corrugated iron. The other main changes are the use of two high gable roofs in place of three low pitched roofs and a dramatic increase in ventilators with rows of tall vents linked to smoke troughs running the full length of each road. Large cowl type ventilators are fitted along the centre line of each roof. Also worth noting is the standard GWR pattern combined water tower and coaling stage on the left of the picture.
[*E N Kneale*]

16. Oswestry Shed, c.1900
In this view it is not readily apparent that the two roads on the right are a later addition as the decorative brickwork extends across all six roads. However, close inspection reveals various differences including the smoke vents in the roof, the use of lead flashing instead of ridge tiles and a steel joist across the doorway instead of arched brickwork. The two locomotives standing outside the shed are Cambrian 4-4-0s 70 and 71 built in 1894 by Sharp, Stewart & Co.
[*M E Lloyd Collection*]

17. Oswestry Shed, c.1963
A close up view of the two road section of the shed showing the inspection pits and a run down collection of locomotives including GWR 0-4-2T 1438 and 'Castle' 4-6-0 7033 *Hartlebury Castle*.
[*E N Kneale*]

18. Oswestry Shed, c.1960
A superb shot of GWR 'Manor' 4-6-0 7819 *Hinton Manor* with every detail picked out in the light from the shed entrance. The smoke troughs can be clearly seen in the roof space.
[*E N Kneale*]

19. Oswestry Shed, c.1960
From the inside looking out, GWR 'Manor' 4-6-0 7822 *Foxcote Manor* stands outside the two road section of the shed while being prepared for duty. The locomotive's cylinder drain cocks are most definitely open!
[*E N Kneale*]

20. Oswestry Shed, c.1963
A close up view of the coaling stage and ash pit with LMS Ivatt Class 2 2-6-0 46514 on the ash pit road. A wagon of ash stands to the left of the locomotive.
[*Brian Taylor*]

21. Oswestry Shed, c.1963
GWR 'County' 4-6-0 1002 *County of Berks* stands at the back of the shed with its motion stripped down for repair.
[*E N Kneale*]

22. Oswestry Shed, c.1960
Another facility of the shed was its turntable, here being used by GWR 'Manor' 4-6-0 7822 *Foxcote Manor*.
[*E N Kneale*]

23. Oswestry Shed, 1951
A view of the sidings behind the shed were a collection of GWR locomotives await their next movements. From right to left they are 0-6-0PT 7434, 'Dean Goods' 0-6-0 2407 and 0-6-0PTs 3767 & 4611.
[*R W Hinton*]

24. Oswestry Shed, 1932
GWR 0-6-0T 1376 pauses alongside the coaling stage between shunting duties. Originally built for the Bristol & Exeter Railway, the locomotive also saw service on the Weymouth Quay line.
[*The late H C Casserley*]

25. Oswestry Shed, 1926
GWR 'Dean Goods' 0-6-0 2457 stands on the ash pit road with the water tank to the right.
[*The late H C Casserley*]

26. Oswestry Shed, c.1963
An unusual shot taken from the tender of GWR 'Castle' 4-6-0 7033 *Hartlebury Castle* parked at the rear of the shed. To the immediate left of the locomotive are the running lines and beyond them are wagons in the works sidings. A GWR 0-6-0PT and 0-4-2T stand to the right while behind them against the shed wall can be seen the shed's stationary boiler.
[E N Kneale]

27. Oswestry Shed, 1926
GWR 'Duke' 4-4-0 3280 *Tregenna* stands outside the shed on a sunny August day while its crew pose for the photographer. Of note is the fire devil provided to keep the water column from freezing in cold weather.
[*The late H C Casserley*]

28. Oswestry Works, 1963
An unusual visitor to the locomotive works was this former Glasgow & South Western Railway 0-6-0T. Built by North British in Glasgow in 1917, it worked in Scotland before being sold by the LMS in 1934 for industrial use at Hafod Colliery near Wrexham. After withdrawal in 1961 it was transferred to Oswestry for storage in 1962 before ultimately moving back to Glasgow for display in the city's transport museum.
[*E N Kneale*]

29. Oswestry Works, c.1960
Most of the works buildings are visible in this view which also shows a GWR 0-6-0PT on pilot duties.
[*Brian Taylor*]

30. Oswestry Works, 1963
This view of the forge in the carriage & wagon works is full of interesting detail. The craftsman is leaning against a hydraulic press and around the walls are a number of hearths. Lengths of chain, buffers and other sundry items are stacked by the hearths while behind the ladder to the left are a quantity of wagon drawhooks. The item prominent in the foreground is an inverted wagon 'W-iron'.
[*E N Kneale*]

31. Oswestry Works, 1963
Another interesting piece of machinery in the works was this large wheel lathe which was belt driven from the overhead shaft, common practice before individual machine tools each had their own electric motors.
[*E N Kneale*]

32. Oswestry Works, 1963
A visitor from Shrewsbury was LMS 'Jubilee' 4-6-0 45572 *Eire* which was receiving attention to its motion.
[*E N Kneale*]

33. Oswestry Works, 1963
The works manager's office contained a fine model of a Cambrian Railways 4-4-0. On the wall behind the model is a blackboard on which are listed the locomotives receiving attention from works staff both in the works itself and at the nearby locomotive shed.
[*E N Kneale*]

34. Oswestry Works, 1959
Welshpool & Llanfair Railway 0-6-0Ts 822 *The Earl* and 823 *The Countess* in storage prior to their return to their home line.
[*Jim Peden*]

35. Oswestry Works, 1963
It was usual practice for locomotives to be separated from their tenders when in works for attention. This separation provides a clear view of the footplate of LMS 'Jubilee' 4-6-0 45572 *Eire* which, from the quantity of firebricks stacked on the footplate, appears to be receiving attention to the brick arch in its firebox.
[*E N Kneale*]

36. Oswestry Works, 1963
One of the works' craftsmen crouched inside the smokebox of GWR 0-6-2T 6625.
[*E N Kneale*]

THE OSWESTRY - GOBOWEN BRANCH

Oswestry first appeared in the title of a proposed railway in June 1845 when parliament authorised the Act for the Shrewsbury, Oswestry & Chester Junction Railway, a line from Ruabon to Shrewsbury which in fact bypassed the town! The proposal was promoted by the directors of the North Wales Mineral Railway whose own line from Wrexham to Chester was authorised in August 1844 and supplemented by a southerly extension to Ruabon authorised in July 1845. The need to serve Oswestry was addressed by a further Act in July 1846 which proposed a branch from Gobowen to Crickheath, south of the town. In fact the line was only built as far as Oswestry and this $2^1/_2$ mile branch opened in December 1848.

After several years of intense railway politics the Shrewsbury & Chester Railway, formed by the amalgamation of the SOCJ and the NWMR by an Act of July 1846, amalgamated with the Great Western Railway in September 1854. At this time the Great Western was still the only railway serving Oswestry, the Oswestry to Pool Quay section of what was to become the Cambrian Railways did not open until May 1860 while the Oswestry, Ellesmere and Whitchurch followed four years later.

Even after the Cambrian Railways became fully established with its Headquarters at Oswestry the GWR retained a separate station, opening a replacement for their original terminus in 1866. Following the Cambrian's amalgamation with the Great Western in 1922 some major modernisation work took place in the Oswestry area. As far as the Gobowen branch was concerned the most important of these was the provision of a north-facing bay platform at the former Cambrian station which allowed the 1866 GWR station to be closed in July 1924 and converted into a goods station, in which role it survived until December 1971.

Passenger services on the Gobowen branch were withdrawn in November 1966, almost two years after the Whitchurch and Welshpool services. There was one intermediate station on the branch, Park Hall Halt, which was opened in 1926 to serve the nearby hospital and remained in use until the withdrawal of passenger services.

The branch remains in place today as part of the freight-only line to ARC's Blodwell Quarry. The last stone trains ran in October 1988 but the branch has been retained for possible future use by block trains of refuse if plans to use the quarry as a landfill site come to fruition.

37. Gobowen, c.1860
Gobowen, on the Shrewsbury to Chester line, was the junction for the Shrewsbury & Chester Railway's short branch to Oswestry. This fine view, taken at the north end of Gobowen station, shows the Italianate style station building and the timber trainshed over the Oswestry branch platform beyond. The period dress of the railway staff and their families is also of interest.
[*Shropshire Records & Research Unit*]

38. Gobowen, 1956
GWR 0-6-0PT 5416 stands in the bay platform at Gobowen at the head of an Oswestry train.
[*H B Priestley - Pacer Archives Collection*]

39. Gobowen, 1969
A view looking towards Shrewsbury showing Gobowen South signal box which controlled the Oswestry branch junction visible just to the left of the warning notice.
[*H B Priestley - Pacer Archives Collection*]

40. Park Hall, c.1960
A view looking towards Oswestry showing the basic facilities at Park Hall Halt. The signal just beyond the road overbridge is the fixed distant for Gobowen South.
[*Lens of Sutton*]

41. Park Hall, c.1965
In the final years of the Gobowen - Oswestry service two car DMUs were used, as typified by this Derby built set leaving Park Hall for Oswestry.
[*M Mensing*]

Map I: GWR Oswestry District, 1943

As noted in the Introduction, the GWR's Oswestry District stretched far beyond the town's boundaries to Pwllheli, Aberystwyth and Brecon. This map, redrawn from the cover of the March 1943 Sectional Appendix, identifies double and single line sections, mineral lines, narrow guage lines and junctions with lines of other districts.

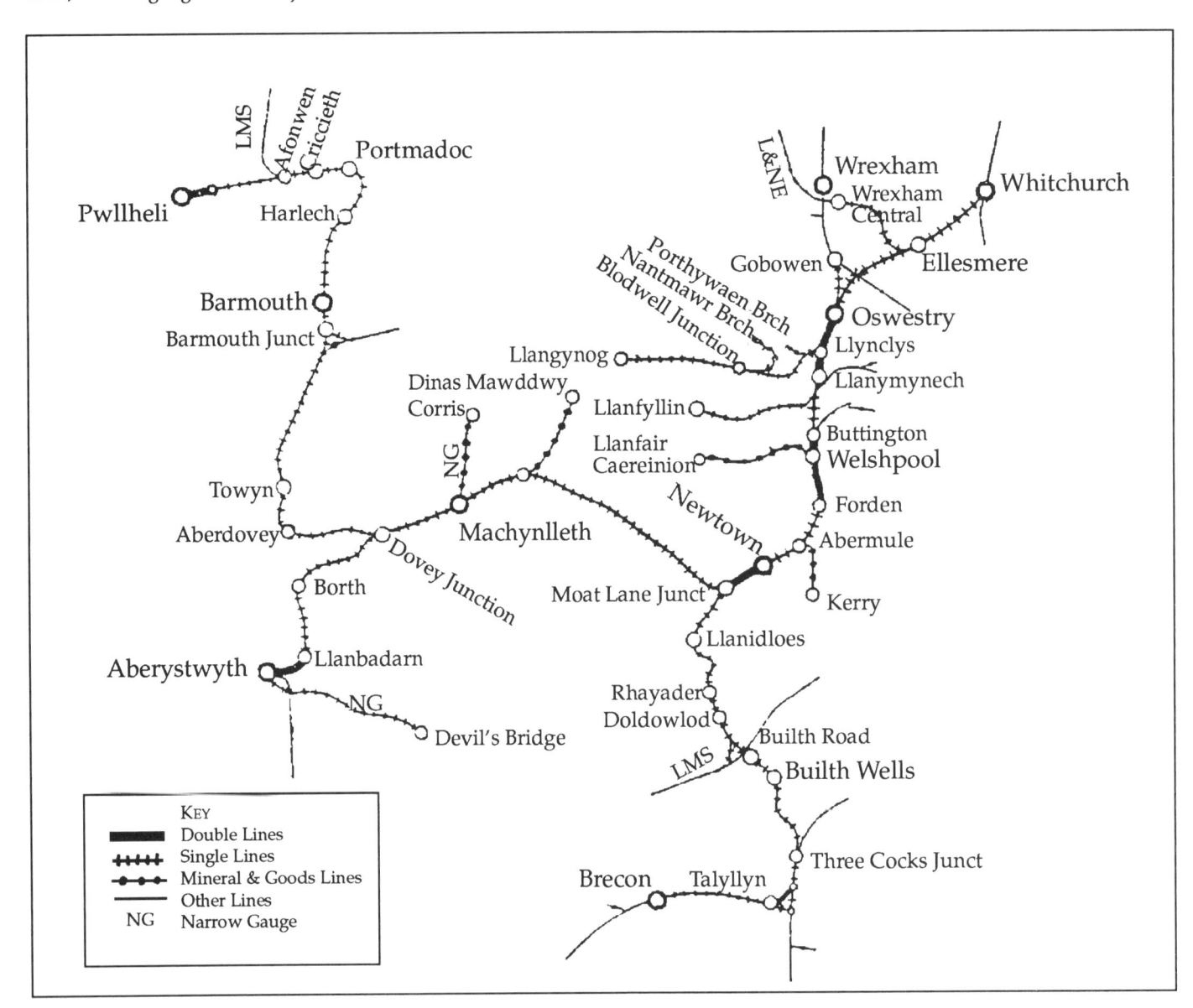

Map II: Lines around Llynclys

The mineral producing area around Llynclys had the most complicated arrangement of lines in the Oswestry area. This diagram attempts to clarify the main details of those lines.

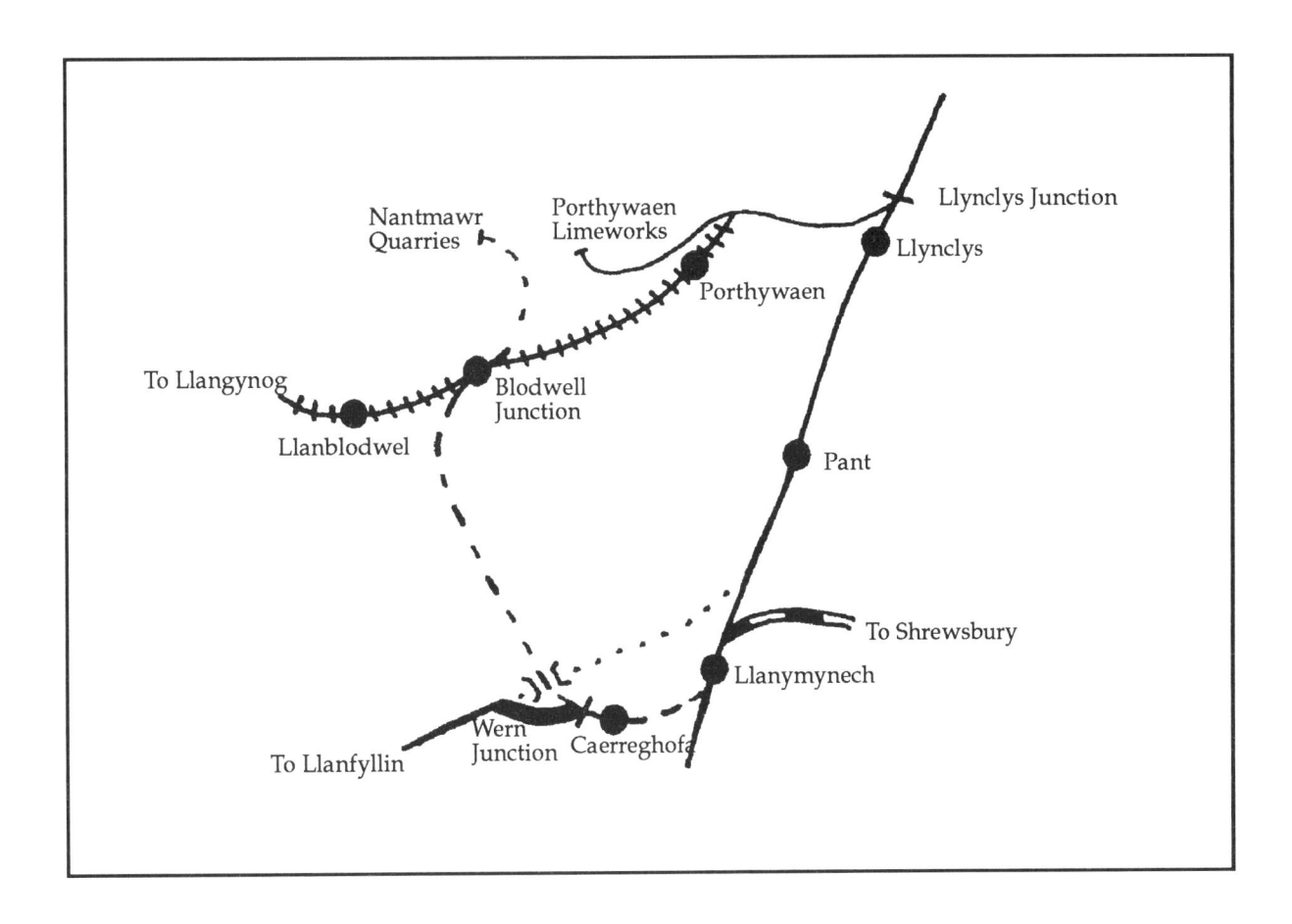

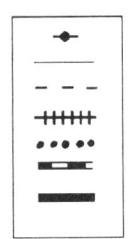

Key

- Stations
- Cambrian Railways
- Potteries, Shrewsbury & North Wales Railway (later leased to the Cambrian Railways)
- Tanat Valley Light Railway
- Original route of Llanfyllin branch
- Potteries, Shrewsbury & North Wales Railway (later Shropshire & Montgomeryshire Light Railway)
- Post 1896 connection to Llanfyllin branch

WHITCHURCH TO WELSHPOOL - THE CAMBRIAN MAIN LINE

The railway between Whitchurch and Welshpool was built during the 1860s by two different railway companies, both of which were based on Oswestry and were to become constituents of the Cambrian Railways.

The Oswestry, Ellesmere & Whitchurch Railway Act received the royal assent on 1 August 1861 with construction work starting soon afterwards. The $10^3/4$ miles from Whitchurch to Ellesmere passed over a three mile stretch of Whixall Moss which presented a major obstacle to construction. The technique of laying bales of brushwood on the moss and building the trackbed above was adopted. Single track was laid on a double line formation and intermediate stations were provided at Welshampton, Bettisfield and Fenn's Bank. The line opened to goods in April 1863 and to passengers the following month.

The section between Ellesmere and Oswestry, construction of which also required peat bogs to be crossed, was provided with an intermediate station at Whittington where the line crossed the Shrewsbury & Chester Railway. The line opened in July 1864, permitting through services to begin between Whitchurch and Oswestry. A station was opened at Frankton in 1866 and a halt was opened at Tinkers Green, between Oswestry and Whittington, in October 1939 to serve the adjacent military facilities.

Ellesmere, the most important intermediate station between Whitchurch and Oswestry, became a junction in November 1895 when a branch to Wrexham via Bangor-on-Dee and Marchwiel was opened. This line is covered in the authors' previous volumes on Wrexham Railways.

The railway between Oswestry and Welshpool was part of the Oswestry & Newtown Railway, the Act for which received the royal assent in June 1855. Construction began at Llanymynech working towards Oswestry. The section between Oswestry and Pool Quay, built as a single track on double line formation, was opened in May 1860. The remainder of the line on to Welshpool, including two crossings of the River Severn, opened in August of the same year. Intermediate stations were provided on opening at Llynclys, Llanymynech, Four Crosses and Pool Quay with Ardleen and Pant added in 1864. The station at Buttington Junction, where the line from Shrewsbury met the Oswestry & Newtown for the parallel run into Welshpool, was opened at the same time as the LNWR (later to become LNWR & GWR joint) line in January 1862. Later improvements included the conversion of the two single lines between Buttington Junction and Welshpool to double track and doubling between Oswestry and Llanymynech.

Both the Oswestry, Ellesmere & Whitchurch and the Oswestry & Newtown became part of the Cambrian Railways on its formation in July 1864. Oswestry became the headquarters of the Cambrian and an important railway centre. In 1922 the Cambrian amalgamated with the Great Western and although the GWR made various improvements the pre-grouping character remained until the early years of the British Railways era. The decision of Beeching's 'Reshaping of British Railways' report to concentrate all traffic to and from the Cambrian Coast via Shrewsbury meant that Whitchurch to Welshpool closed to through traffic during January 1965.

Freight to Ellesmere continued for two more months while the section from Oswestry to Llynclys remains intact to this day as the middle section of what is now a mothballed freight-only branch from Gobowen to ARC's Blodwell Quarry.

42. Whitchurch, 1954
BR Standard Class 4 4-6-0 75023 stands outside Whitchurch shed awaiting its next turn of duty on 27 August 1954.
[*The late H C Casserley*]

43. Whitchurch, c.1960
A view of Whitchurch station looking south towards Shrewsbury. The Cambrian line can just be seen diverging to the right beyond Cambrian Junction signal box. On the platform may be seen a number of racing pigeon baskets awaiting dispatch. The locomotive shed was situated off to the left of the photograph.
[*Lens of Sutton*]

44. Whitchurch, 1959

A fine view of the informative nameboard at the north end of Whitchurch station. GWR 'Manor' 4-6-0 7803 *Barcote Manor* has just arrived with a train from the Cambrian lines. Note in the distance the suspension bridge which carries a footpath over the sidings and running lines.
[*H B Priestley - Pacer Archives Collection*]

45. Fenn's Bank, 1959

Fenn's Bank was the first passing place on the single line from Whitchurch. There was a small goods yard, seen on the right of this view, which dealt primarily with domestic coal and agricultural traffic. At the south end of the station there was a private siding serving the aluminium refinery of H H Wardle (Metals) Ltd.
[*H B Priestley - Pacer Archives Collection*]

46. Bettisfield, 1959
The signalman exchanges tokens with the driver of an Oswestry bound freight despite there being apparatus for the purpose at the bottom of the signal box steps. As at Fenn's Bank there was a loop for passing trains and sidings but only one platform.
[*H B Priestley - Pacer Archives Collection*]

47. Bettisfield, c.1960
A close up of the station building and its raised letter nameboard. The advertising posters encourage travel to Prestatyn and the Isle of Man.
[*Lens of Sutton*]

48. Bettisfield, 1962
A limited stop service from Whitchurch to Welshpool hauled by GWR 2-6-0 6378 stands in the platformless loop at Bettisfield while GWR 'Manor' 4-6-0 7803 *Barcote Manor* runs in past the signal box and token exchange apparatus with a local train for Whitchurch. [*M A King*]

49. Welshampton, c.1910
The local coal merchant is about to load his cart with Staffordshire coal from two wagons standing on the single siding provided at Welshampton. Some of the station buildings may be seen behind the wagons while the station house is just visible to the extreme right.
[Lens of Sutton]

50. Welshampton, c.1960
A close up of the station house at Welshampton which was rented to a railway employee. At the far end of the house may be seen a gate by which passengers gained access to the platform from the road while just visible to the right under the bridge is the ground frame which controlled access to the siding.
[H B Priestly - Pacer Archives Collection]

51. Ellesmere, 1962
GWR Collett 0-4-2 1438 waits at Ellesmere with a train for Wrexham formed of a single autocoach on 26 May 1962.
[*M A King*]

52. Frankton, c.1910
A view of the rather grand station house at Frankton. On the end wall nearest the photographer may be seen the embossed brick Cambrian Railways coat of arms. A closer view of which is reproduced as the frontispiece of this book.
[*Lens of Sutton*]

53. Frankton, 1962

By the time this photograph was taken Frankton station had been demoted to the status of a Halt. LMS Ivatt Class 2 2-6-0 46507 arrives with a two coach local working.
[*H B Priestley - Pacer Archives Collection*]

54. Whittington, c.1959

The Cambrian station at Whittington was known as 'High Level' to distinguish it from the 'Low Level' station below it on the Shrewsbury - Chester line. The Cambrian station closed in January 1960, five years before the line itself. In this view the signal box on the platform provided to control the passing loop can be clearly seen. Goods traffic was not handled but a solitary wagon can be seen in the short siding beyond the platforms.
[*Lens of Sutton*]

55. Tinkers Green, c. 1960
Tinkers Green Halt was situated approximately half way between Whittington and Oswestry and was provided primarily to serve the adjacent army camp. The timber-edged platform and basic buildings may be clearly seen. Short passenger workings were provided between Oswestry and Tinkers Green and were operated according to special working instructions which allowed trains to return to Oswestry without having passed all the way through the single line section to Whittington.
[*Stations UK*]

56. Llynclys, 1958
GWR 2-6-0 6335 arrives at the well kept Llynclys station with a train for Welshpool. In the background can be seen Llynclys Junction where the Tanat Valley line diverged.
[*H B Priestley - Pacer Archives Collection*]

57. Llynclys, 1961
A view showing the main station building. The small shelter opposite has been rebuilt since the previous photograph was taken. Just beyond the overbridge can be seen one of the abutments of the Crickheath Tramway bridge while beyond it is a hut housing a ground frame which controlled access to a siding known as 'Haystack Siding'.
[*Stations UK*]

58. Llynclys, 1963
A view looking towards Welshpool showing the Crickheath Tramway bridge abutments in the foreground. 'Haystack Siding', which was situated to the right of the line just beyond the abutment has been lifted but the Warehouse on the opposite side of the line is still rail served.
[*Mike Lloyd*]

59. Pant, 1963

A view of the signal box and platforms at Pant station. A single goods siding was also provided. Treadle worked bells were provided on either side of the station to warn the porter signalman on duty of approaching trains.
[*H B Priestley - Pacer Archives Collection*]

60. Pant, c.1920

A view looking across the Shropshire Union Canal towards Pant station where the level crossing gates and signal box may be clearly seen. Below the signal box can be seen the small arch of the bridge through which passed a narrow gauge tramway from the quarries at Crickheath Hill. The narrow boat is probably awaiting a cargo of local stone.
[*John Ryan Collection*]

61. Llanymynech, c.1910
A good clear view of Llanymynech station showing the Cambrian Railways building adorned with posters and advertisements of the period and a confectionery machine. The goods yard behind contains an assortment of buildings and wagons. In the distance can be seen Llanymynech Hill with evidence of extensive quarrying clearly visible.
[*Lens of Sutton*]

62. Llanymynech, 1932
A former Cambrian 0-6-0, by now GWR 849, passes Llanymynech southbound. On the right are the sidings of the Shropshire & Montgomeryshire Railway while behind the train another freight may be seen shunting in the yard. The nameboard advises travellers to change at Llanymynech for Llanfyllin.
[*The late H C Casserley*]

63. Llanymynech, 1931

Llanymynech looking south towards Welshpool. The line diverging to the right is the Llanfyllin branch while the wagons are standing on the Shropshire & Montgomeryshire Railway's lines. The signalling is that installed by the Cambrian Railways.
[R S Carpenter]

64. Four Crosses, 1963

This view of Four Crosses shows the staggered platforms and the GWR signal box situated adjacent to the barrow crossing between the two platforms. The goods yard was situated off to the left of the picture. An interesting special instruction applicable to Four Crosses was that because the platform under the road bridge was only three feet wide, the Station Master was responsible for placing a member of staff there when long passenger trains called in order to "caution passengers against passing along".
[H B Priestley - Pacer Archives Collection]

65. Four Crosses, c.1910

Four Crosses station with a freight train passing. The wagons include two from Black Park Colliery at Ruabon and a roofed lime wagon. The goods yard crane and associated buildings can be seen to the left of the station building. Similarities may be seen between this building and that at Welshampton.
[*Lens of Sutton*]

66. Ardleen, 1965

Access to the short platform at Ardleen was by a path from the road overbridge. This view taken shortly after closure shows the very basic facilities and fittings provided.
[*Mike Lloyd*]

67. Pool Quay, c.1900
A very clear view looking south showing the station buildings and the different methods of construction of the two platforms; the passing loop and wooden platform on the right having been added in 1898.
[*Lens of Sutton*]

68. Buttington, c.1955
GWR 'Dukedog' 4-4-0 9001 heads through Buttington with a special working, possibly a troop train, formed of former Southern Railway stock. Ornamental bargeboards are a prominent architectural feature of the station house.
[*R K Blencowe*]

69. Buttington, c.1930
A train for Shrewsbury leaves Buttington. The way in which both the Shrewsbury and Oswestry lines became single immediately beyond the station is apparent in this view.
[*Stations UK*]

70. Buttington Crossing, c.1962

When Buttington Crossing became the junction for the Oswestry and Shrewsbury lines a new British Railways Western Region style signal box was provided. The locomotive running light engine is a GWR Collett 14xx 0-4-2T.
[*H B Priestley - Pacer Archives Collection*]

71. Welshpool, 1956

The revitalization of the Festiniog and Talyllyn Railways by enthusiasts in the 1950s brought some interesting workings to the Cambrian system. It became something of a tradition on the occasion of each Society's AGM for a special train originating in Birmingham or even London and hauled by an unusual locomotive to run to Porthmadog or Tywyn respectively conveying members to the meeting. On 22 September 1956 the Talyllyn special, seen here taking water at Welshpool, was headed by a South Eastern & Chatham Railway D Class 4-4-0 31075 and a GWR 'Dean Goods' 0-6-0 2538.
[*R K Blencowe*]

72. Welshpool, 1936
GWR 'Duke' 4-4-0 3252 *Duke of Cornwall* leaving Welshpool with a train for the Cambrian Coast. The piles of logs in the background are a reminder that the last railborne freight to Welshpool was timber, the traffic lasting well into the mid 1980's.
[*F K Davis*]

73. Welshpool, 1958
An overall view of Welshpool looking east. GWR 2-6-0 6378 is moving through the station 'light engine' while GWR 'Manor' 4-6-0 7803 *Barcote Manor* is standing at the island platform with a train of four corridor coaches. The Welshpool bypass now runs through the station area seen here and the railway has been displaced to the extreme right of the picture where a new island platform has been provided. The station building survives in private hands while the footbridge has been given a new lease of life at Glyndyfrdwy station on the Llangollen Railway.
[*H B Priestley - Pacer Archives Collection*]

74. Welshpool, 1992
A view of Welshpool looking west showing the station area cleared as construction of the town's bypass begins. The new island platform is off the picture to the left.
[*Dave Southern*]

THE LLANFYLLIN BRANCH

The town of Llanfyllin can claim early commuting links with Oswestry. In August 1860 the landlord of the Red Lion Inn, Mr Edward Lloyd, began an omnibus service linking the town with certain morning and evening trains at Llanymynech on the newly opened Oswestry & Newtown Railway.

In September of that year, a preliminary prospectus was issued for the West Midland, Shrewsbury and Coast of Wales Railway, a grand scheme to link the Shrewsbury & Welshpool and the Severn Valley Railways via Llanymynech, thence "near Llanfyllin" and Llanrhaiadr-ym-Mochnant to Llangynog and through the Berwyn mountains to Llandrillo. From there it would have a short branch to Corwen for connection with other lines already authorised. The residents of Llanfyllin were luke-warm to such a scheme, favouring a straightforward branch connection with the Oswestry & Newtown line at Llanymynech. At a public meeting called in October 1860 a committee was formed to progress such a project and a subscription list received an early pledge of £1,000 from Lord Powis and £500 from Mr D Pugh, the local MP. Other local committees set up in Llanymynech, Meifod and Llansaintffraid simultaneously pledged support.

The sod-cutting ceremony took place at Llanfyllin in September 1861 and featured those things which were by now becoming traditional at such events – triumphal arches and processions by all the local military and civil organisations supported by their bands and regalia. The contractor, that stalwart of Cambrian lines Thomas Savin, presented a silver barrow and spade to Mrs Dugdale, wife of the High Sheriff of Montgomeryshire, who had consented to cut the first sod. A meal for four hundred supporters followed at the Wynnstay Arms; the local children received tea and buns and the day concluded with a firework display staged by Messrs Goodby and Darlington of Shrewsbury.

The Act authorising the line received the royal assent in May 1861 but the survey conducted by Messrs R & B Piercy, engineers to the Oswestry and Newtown Railway, had been delayed until "after the harvest to avoid damage to crops". By December, however, the navvies were at work and early in 1862 the local press were announcing that a carriage would operate on the line as far as Llansaintffraid to connect with the omnibus from Llanfyllin which would then be able to make an additional round trip.

An 0-6-0 saddle tank locomotive, *Nant Clwyd*, was the first of its kind to reach Llanfyllin, doing so during March 1863 to be greeted by a large turnout of the inhabitants. The first passenger journey took place during the following month when Mr & Mrs Dugdale, their family and entourage completed a nine hour transit from Brighton. This must surely rank as one of the more unusual through carriage workings!

One evening early in June a special train ran from Llanymynech to Llanfyllin one evening for the benefit of persons attending a concert in aid of Bwlch-y-cibau Church, returning later through to Oswestry. This could claim to be the first public train, although the line was not officially inspected and approved by the Board of Trade until later in the month. The official opening took place during July 1863, the day being marked by a day excursion to Borth, "Fares 5s and 2s 6d, including return", was organised to be followed by dinner in a pavilion adjoining the station presided over by Mr Dugdale.

The initial service between Oswestry and Llanfyllin comprised five trains each way daily, the return fare being 1s 9d 3rd class. The opening of the ill-fated Potteries, Shrewsbury and North Wales Railway (referred to elsewhere in this book) in August 1866 gave a temporary boost to traffic by offering a direct connection at Llanymynech to Shrewsbury.

Traffic on the line was also enhanced in 1881 by the commencement of construction of the Vyrnwy reservoir. A special train ran from Birkenhead Woodside conveying the dignitaries from Liverpool Corporation, who were joined by a party of local worthies at Oswestry. It is recorded that at Llanfyllin they transferred to thirty conveyances, presumably horse-drawn, to proceed to the foundation stone ceremony. Llanfyllin subsequently became the railhead for materials bound for the site and a stable of 95 heavy horses was maintained for this task.

Completion of the reservoir at Lake Vyrnwy led to the development of excursion traffic and this remained important throughout the life of the line. In the Victorian and Edwardian eras the 'Sunday School Outing' reigned supreme. By the 1950s it was the turn of the ramblers and hikers, for whom special trains were laid on.

In 1922 the name of Llansaintffraid station was amended to Llansantffraid. This was the year the Cambrian Railways amalgamated with the Great Western Railway. Nationalisation in 1948 took the branch into the Western Region of British Railways, but initially observers would have noted little change. In the early 1960s LMS designed Ivatt 2-6-0 locomotives were allocated to Oswestry Shed and became the regular motive power for the line in its final years. BR developed this type of engine as the Standard Class 2 2-6-0 and examples of these were also seen.

A steady pattern of travel between Llanfyllin and Oswestry was to remain throughout the life of the branch and even in its closing years the Saturday traffic was considerable. In January 1965 the branch became another victim of Dr Beeching's s axe after completing over a century of service to the towns and villages along its route.

75. Carreghofa, c.1960
The first stopping place after leaving Llanymynech was Carreghofa Halt, which was opened by the GWR in April 1938. In this view looking west the unusual double bridge which carried the road and the Shropshire Union canal over the railway can be seen. Just beyond the Halt was the site of the former Nantmawr Junction, where the Llanymynech loop line originally diverged towards Blodwell Junction.
[*Lens of Sutton*]

76. Llansantffraid, c.1960
Just before arrival at Llansantffraid there was a level crossing over the Llandrinio road which was fully protected by signals controlled from this signal box.
[*Mike Lloyd*]

77. Llansantffraid, c.1900
This early view of the station shows the spelling which prevailed until 1922. Enamel advertising signs feature prominently. The structure is quite substantial with a two-storey Stationmaster's house and a single storey wing providing the station accommodation. The architecture is typical Cambrian cottage style and the gable barge boards are especially decorative.
[*Lens of Sutton*]

78. Llansantffraid, c.1960
A Llanfyllin bound train arriving at Llansantffraid hauled by an LMS Ivatt Class 2 2-6-0 running tender-first. The signalman and driver are about to change the token for the single line from Llanymynech for a tablet which was applicable for the rest of the journey to Llanfyllin. The line in the left foreground is the Up crossing loop, which also gave access to sidings and a warehouse which was used primarily for agricultural traffic.
[*Authors' Collection*]

79. Llansantffraid, c.1955
Another view of a token/tablet exchange at Llansantffraid with a three coach train hauled by GWR Collett 0-4-2T 5806. The line was originally controlled by the tablet system throughout, but the electric token for the lower section was introduced following alterations at Llanymynech by the GWR. This view demonstrates the rural idyll of the branch railway station with its flower beds and general tidiness.
[*Authors' Collection*]

80. Llanfechain, c.1960
An unidentified Class 2 2-6-0 locomotive and its two coach train arriving at Llanfechain from Oswestry. Note the coal merchant's lorry as well as a fine example of a Leyland HGV parked in the station yard. It is recorded that there was once a signal box here situated behind the station nameboard but it is uncertain if it was ever a block post.
[H B Priestley - Pacer Archives Collection]

81. Bryngwyn, c.1890
Bryngwyn, although described as a station in this early view, displays the characteristics of a request stop with a signal for operation by intending passengers who wished to stop a train. The signal was removed in the 1920s after which trains made a regular stop. In the early days of the railway this location was known as Brongwyn.
[John Ryan Collection]

82. Llanfyllin, 1950

GWR Collett 0-4-2T 5806 is seen after arrival at Llanfyllin with a short train whose pristine stock apppears to be direct from the paint shop. The effects of nationalisation were resisted on the Western Region and these coaches appear to be in the best traditions of 'chocolate and cream' complete with white roofs. Regrettably the locomotive does not match these standards. Note the locomotive shed at the far end of the yard.
[W A Camwell]

83. Llanfyllin, 1962

In the early 1960s the 2-6-0s were the staple motive power on the branch. Here 46509 'blows off' awaiting departure with a two coach train. Closure is still over two years away but the station area is beginning to look a little unkempt. The identity or purpose of the man in front of the train is not known, but he clearly pre-dates the era of high visibility orange vests!
[H B Priestley - Pacer Archives Collection]

84. Llanfyllin, 1932
In this delightful scene of 30 years earlier wooden four wheeled coaches befitting a branch line of the period are evident. The 'period' passengers are also worthy of closer scrutiny.
[*The late H C Casserley*]

RAILWAYS IN THE TANAT VALLEY

As noted when considering the Llanfyllin branch, a route through the Tanat Valley had been proposed in the prospectus for the West Midlands, Shrewsbury and Coast of Wales Railway in 1860. There had been a variety of earlier schemes for routes through Mid and North Wales but their objective had been to secure a route and a port for Irish traffic, rather than considering any local needs. Two locations, Porth Dinllaen and Holyhead, vied for the distinction of being the Irish port. Routes to both presented considerable engineering obstacles but Holyhead and the route from Chester along the coast of North Wales and across Anglesey was ultimately favoured.

The subsequent development of railways in the Tanat Valley, however, is linked to more local issues, primarily the exploitation of minerals in the area prompted initially by the railhead established at Porthywaen in 1863 as a branch from the Oswestry and Newtown Railway. There had been numerous tramroads established in the eighteenth and early nineteenth centuries in the Llanymynech and Porthywaen areas as feeders for mineral traffic to the Montgomery and Ellesmere (later Shropshire Union) canals and the development of new rail links was a natural progression.

The next important development of a mineral line after the Porthywaen branch was the Nantmawr branch of the Potteries, Shrewsbury and North Wales Railway from Llanymynech. However, as we will see later the 'Potts' line, as it had become known, was in difficulties by 1880 and the owner of the Nantmawr quarries, Mr France, was soon appealing to the Cambrian Railways to operate and maintain the line. In 1896 the Cambrian opened a new connection between the Nantmawr branch and the Llanfyllin branch which had the additional benefit of improving the working of Llanfyllin line trains at Llanymynech which had previously had to reverse up a gradient before starting on their journey.

However, standard gauge railways with both their physical and legal constraints were not an ideal response to the flexible needs of quarrying and mining, particularly in more isolated areas, and it was really the passing of the Light Railways Act of 1896 that made the expansion of industries further up the Tanat Valley a more attractive proposition. The Act empowered local councils to support light railway schemes in their areas and had additional benefits in securing Treasury grants and loans and minimising opposition from local landowners.

In 1897 the Cambrian's chief engineer, George Owen, provided his services to the promoters of the Tanat Valley Railway. His proposals were presented to the Light Railway Commissioners in Oswestry in August 1897 and an Order was granted the following month despite a rival bid from promoters of a narrow gauge line from Llanfyllin to Llangynog.

The traditional sod-cutting ceremony with associated festivities was carried out at Porthywaen in September 1899 by the Countess of Powis. A mere ten days later cost estimates began to rise as the lowest tender received for building the line, that of Messrs Strachan of Cardiff, was approximately £1,000 higher than the estimates. Increased loans were secured from both the Treasury and Liverpool Corporation, whose interest had previously been secured because of the new railway's potential in assisting their construction scheme for a pipeline from Lake Fyrnwy to proposed filter beds at Oswestry.

Construction of the line began in July 1901 but was beset by bad weather and difficulties with the contractor, who even began to operate his own unofficial passenger service between Llangynog and Porthywaen! Completion was ultimately achieved and the opening ceremony was performed in January 1904 by the Dowager Lady Williams Wynn. There were stations at Porthywaen, Blodwell Junction, Llanyblodwel, Llansilin Road, Llangedwyn, Pentrefelin, Llanrhaiadr-Mochant, Pedairfford, Penybontfawr and Llangynog. Llangedwyn and Llanrhaiadr had two platforms with passing loops and open lever frames located on a simple plinth at the end of one of the platforms. The only signalboxes were at Blodwell Junction and Porthywaen, the latter being reduced to ground frame status in the 1930s. In true light railway fashion the stations had the simplest of timber framed and corrugated sheeted structures. The final construction bill was in excess of £92,000 and double the original estimates. A receiver was appointed in April 1904 and the company remained in receivership until taken over by the Cambrian in March 1921.

In addition to being the first Welsh light railway, the Tanat Valley line was also claimed to be the first bona-fide light railway in Britain, since its nearest rival at that time (in Scotland) was a commercial line which was not a public railway.

This quaint line with its occasional mixed trains and distinctive motive power operated until the constraints of the Second World War reduced the passenger service which was not fully restored post-war. The rival road service of Crosville Motor Services soon established a toe-hold and the line closed to passengers in 1951 to be followed in 1952 by withdrawal of the freight services beyond Llanrhaiadr-Mochant. In December 1960 flood damage to the piers of a river bridge west of Llangedwyn led to the line being cut back to Blodwell Junction.

The remaining traffic was stone from Nantmawr and Blodwell quarries. Traffic from Nantmawr ceased in the early 1970s but that from Blodwell, mainly ballast for British Rail, continued until 28 October 1988.

It is perhaps ironic that reversals of mineral train workings was one of the early difficulties besetting the branch lines radiating from Llanyblodwell and Llanymynech and resulted in a variety of proposals for routeing, the complexities of which are outside of the scope of this book. It is perhaps suffice to record that many of the difficulties appear to have been generated by a local landowner, Viscount Newport, fourth Earl of Bradford, who had vested interests in the Shropshire Railways Company. The Town Clerk of Oswestry, Joseph Parry-Jones, was also the solicitor to the Tanat Valley Railway and there was much acrimonious correspondence between him and the Shropshire Railways solicitors in London . Much of the argument centred around the need, or otherwise, for a fly-over to enable the Tanat Valley line to cross the Nantmawr branch and it was not until 1898, when the Cambrian acquired a lease on the Nantmawr line, that the fly-over plan was finally abandoned. Allied to these arguments was another controversy concerning through workings between Llangynog and Llanymynech which would have necessitated construction of a 'west curve' creating a triangular junction at Llanyblodwel. Initially this was overcome by an agreement that a through carriage would be attached and detached at the reconstructed Llanyblodwel PSNW station. Few passengers made use of this facility which was withdrawn in January 1917. The Earl of Bradford made a final attempt in 1906 to get the west curve built but the Cambrian continued to prevaricate until the original agreement ran out in 1921. The west curve was never built and the remainder of the Llanymynech loop line, as it had become known, became disused after about 1925 and was lifted by 1938.

85. Llynclys Junction, 1904

The Tanat Valley line left the Oswestry to Welshpool main line at Llynclys Junction, seen here in Cambrian Railways days with their distinctive signals much in evidence. Originally this had been the starting point for the Porthywaen branch and at that time was known as Porthywaen Junction. The junction was sited a few chains north of Llynclys station. The rather diminutive signal box, which was dwarfed further by the adjacent water tower, also served the marshalling sidings which developed on both sides of the main line.
[*John Ryan Collection*]

86. Porthywaen, 1961
The first halt on the Tanat valley branch to Llangynog was at Porthywaen. Views taken at intermediate stations during its passenger service days are rare but this view is illustrative of of the style of short concrete faced platform which was repeated along the line. Originally the simple clinker and ash platform had been retained by heavy timbers but the Cambrian began a programme of replacement with concrete as early as 1920. In its original state this platform also boasted a simple corrugated waiting shelter and office and there was a primitive gents urinal at the bottom of the ramp at the signal box end. A pannier tank locomotive can just be seen behind the signal box. A number of mineral branches serving quarries, lime kilns and a wagon repair works diverged here on varying gradients.
[*Stations UK*]

87. Porthywaen, c.1935
A view of Porthywaen, taken about 1935. The locomotive is GWR 2-4-0 1308 *Lady Margaret*, (acquired by the GWR when it took over the Liskeard and Looe Railway in Cornwall in 1909). It was obviously ideal for light railway work and was transferred to Oswestry shortly after the Grouping of 1923. The train here is heading towards Llynclys from Whitehaven Quarry. The wagon repair works can be seen behind the train. In the centre of the picture is the narrow gauge track of the Crickheath Tramway, which crossed the Tanat Valley line at this point and followed into the Quarry as mixed gauge track. In later years the narrow gauge line was removed and a standard gauge crossover to the 'main' line was installed. The signal box was reduced to ground frame status around this period. [*M E M Lloyd Collection*]

88. Porthywaen, c.1960
A different view of the platform at Porthywaen, this time looking west towards the level crossing over the main Llanfyllin road. Ironically, even when Porthywaen signal box was fully operational, there were no signals to protect the crossing, the principal role of the signal box being to provide protection where the Crickheath tramway crossed.
[*Lens of Sutton*]

89. Porthywaen, c.1985
A BR Class 25 diesel locomotive crosses the A495 at Porthywaen at the head of a BR ballast train from ARC's Blodwell Quarry. Note that although there were gates across the railway they were set back slightly from the road and when open for rail traffic they were swung clear of the track but did not protect the road, that duty being the responsibility of the two flagmen seen here.
[*Dave Southern*]

90. Blodwell Junction, c.1960
A view looking east at Blodwell Junction towards Llanddu, where the line to Nantmawr diverged. The construction of the A495 road overbridge is rather unusual.
[Lens of Sutton]

91. Blodwell Junction, 1957
Ivatt Class 2 2-6-0 46513 on a short freight train at Blodwell Junction. The occasion seems to have coincided with some localised flooding. The home signal from Llanrhaiadr Mochnant direction can be seen still 'off'. The former Llanymynech loop, by this time reduced to a siding, diverges to the left.
[N C Simmons]

92. Blodwell Junction, c.1955

Another view of Blodwell Junction in busier times with LMS Ivatt Class 2 2-6-0 46511 in charge. The rural setting is well portrayed and the mixed nature of the traffic is evidenced by box vans, cattle trucks, a container flat and ballast hoppers. [*The late C E Stephens*]

93. Llansilin Road, c.1965

The next stop on the line was at Llansilin Road which in its heyday was well equipped for freight traffic. In addition to the loop line there was a small warehouse, cattle dock and weighbridge facility. Penybontfawr, between Llanrhaiadr Mochnant and Llangynog had similar arrangements.
[*Lens of Sutton*]

94. Llangedwyn, 1958
Llangedwyn was originally a tablet station and passing place but the loop here was cut back to form a siding in 1922 and the tablet section became Blodwell Junction to Llanrhaiadr Mochnant.
[*The late H C Casserley*]

95. Llanrhaiadr Mochnant, 1944
Mr W E Morris (Station Master) and son at the open ground frame which worked the station's points and signals. Did this early training for Morris junior. result in succession to railway service, once a tradition in many families?
[*MEM Lloyd Collection*]

96. Llanrhaiadr Mochnant, c.1957
Ivatt Class 2 locomotive 2-6-0 46513 is seen here shunting the yard at Llanrhaiadr Mochnant. This scene is post 1952, by whch time this location had become the railhead for the remaining freight traffic.
[*N C Simmons*]

97. Llanrhaiadr Mochnant, 1958
Llanrhaiadr Mochnant on 20 September 1958, the occasion of a special passenger working organised by the Midlands Area of the Stephenson Locomotive Society which covered both the Tanat Valley and the Llanfyllin branches in the light of rumours that closure of the latter was being considered. This train started from Gobowen, after arrival of connections from Stratford-on-Avon and Birmingham. The fare from Birmingham was 18s 6d (92.5p).
[*The late H C Casserley*]

98. Llangynog, 1947
Llangynog was the terminus of the Tanat Valley line. In this view can be seen, from left to right, the booking office and waiting room, the goods warehouse and the facilities for gentlemen. The ladies toilet was contained in the small extension to the waiting room which had the 'convenience' of being offset from the platform, particularly since the facility was of the 'privy' type which required access underneath for emptying!
[IRS Ken Cooper Collection]

99. Llangynog, c.1952
Llangynog originally had its own engine shed. To the right of this view can be seen the water tank and the inspection pit. In the right foreground the brick floor indicating the location of the shed can just be discerned.
[MEM Lloyd Collection]

100. Llangynog, c.1947
GWR 2-4-0T 1196 stands on the head shunt while running round its train at Llangynog. 1196 and her sister engine 1197 were GWR rebuilds of Cambrian engines 58 & 59 which had been originally built in 1866 and had worked the line since its opening. In this rebuilt form they survived the nationalisation to join the British Railways fleet before being withdrawn in April 1948, surely an incredible record.
[*IRS Ken Cooper Collection*]

101. Llangynog, c.1947
GWR 2-4-0T 1196 at Llangynog prior to departure for Oswestry with a train formed of one bogie coach and two four wheeled examples.
[*IRS Ken Cooper Collection*]

The Shropshire & Montgomeryshire Railway

The Main Line

The Shropshire & Montgomeryshire Railway, which wound its way across the Shropshire countryide from Shrewsbury to Llanymynech with branches to Nantmawr and Criggion, has one of the most chequered histories of any line in Britain. In just under 100 years it was opened and closed three times, operated by five different companies, one of which never ran any public trains, and lay dormant for three decades.

Its history began in the 1860s as part of a grand scheme to provide a direct route between the Potteries, Mid Wales and ultimately, via a Cardigan Bay port, Ireland. The two leading participants in the scheme, the Shrewsbury & North Wales Railway (Llanymynech to Redhill (better known as Hookagate)) and the Shrewsbury & Potteries Junction Railway (Redhill to Shrewsbury) amalgamated in July 1866 to form the Potteries, Shrewsbury & North Wales Railway.

Shortly afterwards, in August 1866, the double track line opened throughout between Llanymynech and Shrewsbury for passengers and freight. The line's Shrewsbury terminus was at Abbey Foregate, in the shadow of the Abbey church. A connection to the Shrewsbury to Wellington line was provided running roughly north east from a point a few hundred yards short of the terminus to Potteries Junction, east of Abbey Foregate Junction.

The Company was soon in financial difficulties and the line closed in December 1866. Following a sale of assets which included the singling of the line it reopened two years later. Receipts peaked in 1872 but decline followed, resulting in the appointment of a Receiver in 1877 and closure for a second time in June 1880.

The Shropshire Railways Company was incorporated in August 1888 to resurrect the line but although some engineering work was carried out in 1890 the line was not reopened.

In February 1909, making use of the provisions of the 1896 Light Railways Act, a Light Railway Order gave the Shropshire & Montgomeryshire Light Railway Company powers to rebuild and operate the line which was reopened in April 1911. The Company's engineer was Holman F Stephens, later to be known as Colonel Stephens, a well-known promoter of light railways. Following the First World War traffic declined as passengers turned to motor buses and the road haulage industry, making use of ex-Army lorries, began to compete for goods traffic. Colonel Stephens died in 1931 and regular passenger services ceased in November 1933, although occasional excursions continued until 1937. A residual goods service of one train per day was all that remained and, had it not been for the Second World War, complete closure would have probably followed within five years.

However, the War Department saw the lightly populated countryside through which the line ran as a suitable site for a network of ordnance depots and requisitioned the S&M to serve them. WD operations began in June 1941 and was accompanied by large scale relaying of the main line and construction of many miles of sidings to serve the various depots. WD locomotives and personnel worked all services over the line, including the residual public goods service.

On nationalisation in 1948 the line passed to joint WD and BR control and remained so until 1960 when, in February of that year, WD traffic ceased. BR assumed responsibility for demolition which was completed in 1962. That is not quite the end of the S&M story, however, as the Esso oil terminal at Shrewsbury Abbey received deliveries by rail until July 1988. Since the 1960 closure access to the S&M terminus had been via a connection from the former GWR Severn Valley line.

The Criggion Branch

The history of the Criggion Branch closely mirrors that of the main line. It opened to goods traffic at the same time as the main line and to passengers in June 1871. In the Stephens era the branch reopened to freight in February 1912 and to passengers in August of that year. The branch passenger service was reduced to Saturdays only in 1928 and even these were cut back to Melverley in 1932, due to the condition of the viaduct over the Severn, before final withdrawal in November 1933.

The main source of freight traffic on the branch was Dolerite from the quarry at Criggion, a traffic that continued until December 1959 but which was also disrupted by problems with Melverley Viaduct. Between January 1940 and October 1941 the structure was out of use following ice damage and so the quarry's output was conveyed by road to Four Crosses, south of Llanymynech on the Cambrian main line, for onward dispatch by rail. Further problems occured in 1945 when locomotive movements over the bridge were restricted to those of the quarry company's Sentinel shunter. A new bridge of GWR design was installed in 1948 and still survives as a road bridge. The branch passed to BR on nationalisation and in May 1949 public goods services were withdrawn although stone traffic continued until December 1959.

The Nantmawr Branch

Although this branch was originally part of the Potteries, Shrewsbury & North Wales Railway, its history became so closely entwined with later Cambrian Railways developments in that area that it was considered in the chapter on the Tanat Valley.

102. Shrewsbury Abbey, c.1938
By this date passenger services had ceased but a residual daily freight service still operated. *Hesperus*, a lightweight 0-6-0 originally built by Beyer Peacock of Manchester for the London & South Western Railway in 1875 and purchased by Stephens in 1912, is shunting a former Midland Railway parcels van.
[*Lens of Sutton*]

103. Shrewsbury Abbey, c.1925
Many passenger services in the latter years of the Stephens era were worked by railcar sets such as the one pictured here at Shrewsbury Abbey. Two similar sets were built in 1923, one by Edmunds of Thetford with Ford engines and the other by Wolseley Siddeley.
[*Lens of Sutton*]

104. Meole Brace, c.1915
The station at Meole Brace, a suburb of Shrewsbury, was added during the 1910/11 reconstruction of the line. Note how the station building has been located under the road overbridge to give it additional protection, something made possible by the fact that when originally built the line was double track.
[*Lens of Sutton*]

105. Ford, c.1958
Ford Halt was added by the WD during their period of operation of the S&M to serve the nearby army camp. It was located on the Shrewsbury side of Ford & Crossgates station and consisted of a simple platform of concrete slabs supported on brick piers. In this view WD 9104, a four wheel Drewry railcar is passing the halt while working a railway enthusiasts' special.
[*Lens of Sutton*]

106. Kinnerley, c.1930
Kinnerley was the most important intermediate point on the line, being the junction for Criggion and the site of both the S&M's and later the WD's locomotive sheds. In this view looking towards Llanymynech the ramshackle nature of the S&M is evident with, from left, carriages stabled in the Criggion branch bay platform, a single coach and parcels van at the Llanymynech platform and, almost hidden behind the ground frame hut, one of the railcar sets.
[*Lens of Sutton*]

107. Kinnerley, c.1947
A selection of WD motive power is visible in this view of Kinnerley shed. From left are three Wickham four wheel inspection trollies, a former GWR 'Dean Goods' 0-6-0 and, just visible in the background, two 'Austerity' 0-6-0STs and an ex-GER J69 0-6-0T.
[*Lens of Sutton*]